The Official
Heart of Midlothian
2008 Annual

"The Heart and Soul of Edinburgh"

Written by Final Whistle Media

Roddy Mackenzie/Adriana Wright

Acknowledgements: Michael Mackenzie

Design: David Flockhart

A Grange Publication

© 2007. Published by Grange Communications Ltd., Edinburgh, under licence from Heart of Midlothian Football Club. Printed in the EU.

Photographs © SNS Group

ISBN 978-1-905426-83-6

£6.99

The Heart and Soul of Edinburgh

Contents

Introduction

Welcome to the third full-colour Official Hearts Annual – an essential guide to another dramatic year at the club.

Another historic season saw the club play in the Champions League for the first time and attract bumper crowds to Murrayfield for the ties against Siroki Bijeg and AEK Athens as Hearts' magnificent support once again turned out in force.

The highs and lows of another season are captured in every detail right through to the final day drama at Rugby Park when Hearts were just pipped for a UEFA Cup spot by Aberdeen.

The 2008 annual looks back at that remarkable win over Hibs at Easter Road in March and delves further back into history to highlight the most memorable Hearts' wins at Easter Road. Who can forget Phil Stamp's injury-time winner? Or Wayne Foster's cup cracker that assured him a place in the club's folklore?

Who were Hearts' greatest captains? We look back at a few of the candidates through from Tom Purdie, a founder member of the club, to Dave Mackay, who tasted glory both sides of the border.

And we celebrate some of the great goal-grabbers through the years. Barney Battles, whose league record for a season is set in stone, Jimmy Wardhaugh, whose all-time tally will never be overtaken and John Robertson, whose goals dominated the modern era.

But the 2008 annual does not just deal in past and present as we pick out some of the stars to watch for the future. As well as full profiles of all the current squad, we look at some of the players who are knocking on the door of a first-team place.

From the moment Barcelona set foot in Edinburgh in July, it was clear it was going to be another ground-breaking season for Hearts. Sit back and enjoy another thrilling ride!

Year	Event
1874	founded
1880	record victory, 21-0 v Anchor
1882	record defeat, 1-8 v Vale of Leven
1890	join 11-team inaugural Scottish League
1891	first major trophy, the Scottish Cup
1895	first league championship
1914	First World War, entire first team volunteer to serve country
1931	Barney Battles sets club record of 44 league goals in a season
1932	record Tynecastle crowd of 53,396 watch Scottish Cup tie v Rangers
1939	league suspended due to Second World War
1954	first post-war trophy, the League Cup
1956	first post-war Scottish Cup
1958	league title returns after 61-year absence
1958	made European debut against Belgians Standard Liege and go out 6-3 on aggregate
1960	won last Scottish League title

Tynecastle

Timeline

Year	Event
1965	lose out on league title to Kilmarnock on goal average
1977	relegated from the top flight for the first time
1978	promoted back to Premier League
1979	relegated again
1980	won first division title
1981	finish bottom of Premier League
1983	promoted back to Premier League
1986	miss out on league title to Celtic on goal difference
1989	face Bayern Munich in last eight of UEFA Cup but lose 2-1 on aggregate
1997	John Robertson breaks Jimmy Wardhaugh's league scoring record of 206 goals
1998	end 36 years without a trophy by beating Rangers 2-1 in the Scottish Cup final at Celtic Park
2006	win Scottish Cup after beating Gretna at Hampden on penalties
2006	play in Champions League for the first time
2007	entertain Barcelona at Murrayfield in club's highest-profile friendly

JULY

Dunfermline	1	Hearts	2

Hearts got their SPL campaign off to the perfect start thanks to a late goal from Michal Pospisil which handed them a win at East End Park.

He knocked the ball home 13 minutes from time after Bruno Aguiar's free-kick had come back off the crossbar.

Hearts had made the breakthrough after 14 minutes as Pospisil created the goal with a fine cross from the left which Roman Bednar hooked into the net from six yards.

Dunfermline equalised after 62 minutes when Simmons squeezed home a header at the back post from Scott Muirhead's corner.

Dunfermline's Andy Tod was then dismissed after his second booking for a foul on Julien Brellier.

AUGUST

Hearts	2	Celtic	1

A Roman Bednar double dealt champions Celtic their first defeat of the season as Hearts continued their excellent league form.

Hearts took the lead four minutes into the second half with a well-worked goal. Michal Pospisil freed Bednar and he produced a cool finish to put his side ahead.

However, Celtic scored against the run of play after 65 minutes when they broke quickly from a Hearts corner and Aiden McGeady fed Petrov who produced a terrific left-foot finish.

Then, with just three minutes left, a misplaced pass from Lennon let in Bednar and he rounded Boruc to nab the winning goal.

Hearts	0	Falkirk	0

Hearts failed to break down a well-organised Bairns defence in a bad-tempered clash with Falkirk boss John Hughes sent to the stand after a half-time clash with Michal Pospisil.

Roman Bednar had Hearts' best chance in the first half. He ran on to Karl Dodd's mistake but was foiled when Scott Higgins saved with his feet.

Falkirk also had their chances and Pedro Moutinho wasted a clear opening when Liam Craig's cross found him ten yards out, but he could only volley straight at Craig Gordon.

Hearts pushed hard for a late winner and Pospisil should have netted from Saulius Mikoliunas' cross. Bednar created another chance and blasted a late volley over the bar.

Rangers	2	Hearts	0

A double strike by Kris Boyd early on in the second half gave Rangers a comfortable win over Hearts at Ibrox as Hearts struggled to maintain their early league form.

Craig Gordon performed heroics for Hearts as he raced from his line to block Dado Prso's shot and then reacted well to touch over Boyd's clever overhead flick.

However, Rangers caught Hearts out with two goals inside the first five minutes of the second half when Boyd sent Gordon the wrong way from the penalty spot after Prso had been brought down. Shortly after, Boyd was left unmarked at the back post and headed home a simple goal.

Hearts' discipline cracked under the relentless Rangers pressure and Robbie Neilson saw red in the final minutes for a second bookable offence.

| Hearts | 4 | Inverness CT | 1 |

A makeshift Hearts side rediscovered their form as they battled out a 4-1 win at Inverness to go straight to the top of the SPL.

With Neil McCann causing problems down the left, Hearts went ahead when the winger's low cross was volleyed home by Mauricio Pinilla after 19 minutes.

Caley Thistle netted an equaliser after half-an-hour but Hearts regained the lead three minutes from half time. Hartley's free-kick from the right was met powerfully by Jamie Mole.

In the second half Andrew Driver made no mistake when he capitalised on Ross Tokely's poor clearance to thunder home a close-range volley.

And fellow substitute Bruno Aguiar rounded off the scoring with a header two minutes from time.

SEPTEMBER

| Hearts | 0 | St Mirren | 1 |

St Mirren performed a smash and grab at Tynecastle as they snatched a one-goal victory in a stormy match over a shocked Hearts and climbed to fourth in the table.

Saulius Mikoliunas' low effort was brilliantly turned around the post by Tony Bullock, who then made a superb fingertip save from Steven Pressley's header.

Roman Bednar skipped around Bullock only for Andy Millen to get back and clear off the line.

However, Saints sent Tynecastle silent just eight minutes from the final whistle.

Craig Molloy fired in a powerful shot from 15 yards which Gordon did well to parry but Stewart Kean reacted quickest to prod home and give St Mirren victory.

| Motherwell | 0 | Hearts | 1 |

A Jamie Mole goal midway through the second half handed Hearts victory in a nervous encounter against a struggling Motherwell side.

The best action was actually kept for the four minutes added on, with Richie Foran missing a great chance after he was put clear one on one with the goalkeeper by Marc Fitzpatrick's through ball.

The stalemate ended on 69 minutes when Hearts broke after clearing a Motherwell corner. McCann moved forward quickly before releasing Mole, who rounded Colin Meldrum and eventually shot home past a posse of Well defenders on the line.

Craig Gordon sealed the win for Hearts with two minutes left when he pulled off a stunning one-handed save from Jim Paterson's close-range effort.

| Aberdeen | 1 | Hearts | 3 |

Hearts consolidated their second place in the SPL with a hard-fought win over a determined Aberdeen side at Pittodrie.

Hearts opened the scoring on 64 minutes as Paul Hartley's swerving free kick ricocheted off the shoulder of centre-back Christophe Berra and crept inside the post.

Slick play between Mauricio Pinilla and Saulius Mikoliunas sent the winger clear on the right; his cross was played on by Roman Bednar into the path of Pinilla who gleefully clipped the ball home for the visitors' second goal.

Aberdeen were carved open again minutes later when a precise pass from Pinilla found Mikoliunas who planted the ball behind Jamie Langfield.

Dyron Daal scored a late consolation for Aberdeen.

Hearts	4	Dundee Utd	0

Out of Europe but still very much in the title race, Hearts rode their luck to cruise to a comfortable victory over the Tangerines.

Hearts went ahead with a fortuitous goal as Andrius Velicka's shot took a deflection off full-back Alan Archibald before flying into the net.

Derek Stillie made a superb one-handed save to deny Mirsad Beslija before the Bosnian winger delivered a perfect cross which Juho Makela sidefooted in from close range.

United kept battling, but Archibald's foul on Beslija allowed Paul Hartley to make it 3-0 from the penalty spot and substitutes Roman Bednar and Jamie Mole then combined to leave the latter with a simple tap-in to complete the rout.

OCTOBER

Hibs	2	Hearts	2

Ten-man Hearts staged a magnificent comeback to earn a draw against Hibs in a remarkable Edinburgh derby at Easter Road.

Hibs stormed into an early two-goal lead in the game, but Hearts fought back despite being reduced to ten men with the sending off of Saulius Mikoliunas early in the second half.

Hibs raced into the lead with just four and a half minutes on the clock as Merouane Zemmama scored his first ever goal for the Easter Road side and they stretched their lead on 16 minutes through New Zealand international Chris Killen.

A moment of madness by goalkeeper Zibi Malkowski handed Hearts a lifeline as he came off his line allowing Andrius Velicka to head into an empty net. And Hearts found the vital goal after 72 minutes when Velicka struck for the second time.

Hearts	0	Kilmarnock	2

Hearts lost ground on leaders Celtic as they slipped to defeat against a disciplined Kilmarnock at Tynecastle.

First-half goals from Danny Invincibile and former Heart Gary Wales effectively took the game out of reach of the home side, who did not muster much in the second half.

Hearts were out of the traps quickly and there was an early shout for a penalty after Roman Bednar tumbled in the area under pressure from Graeme Smith, but referee Kenny Clark was not interested.

It was Kilmarnock who took a shock lead after 28 minutes as Steven Naismith waltzed past three defenders, before laying the ball off for Invincibile. Ten minutes later Wales' 20-yard effort took a deflection before beating Craig Gordon.

Hearts	1	Dunfermline	1

Hearts' miserable form continued as they dropped two points against relegation battlers Dunfermline at Tynecastle.

But Hearts were in front after only 12 minutes thanks to a clanger from Roddy McKenzie. The keeper pushed the ball into Paul Hartley's path and his quick back-heel across goal was perfect for Andrius Velicka, who tapped in from close-range.

And only two minutes into the second half Dunfermline were level as Jim Hamilton bundled home Stephen Simmons' downward header.

Hearts dominated in possession terms later on and it took an exceptional goal-line clearance seconds from the end by Andy Tod to earn the Pars a hard-won point, as he headed Robbie Neilson's shot over the bar.

NOVEMBER

Celtic	2	Hearts	1

Celtic staged an incredible fightback with two goals in the last five minutes as they avoided dropping points against Hearts for the second time in the season.

Things looked promising for Hearts when they took the lead through a goal from Andrius Velicka with 18 minutes to go.

However, when substitute Jiri Jarosik headed in a Shunsuke Nakamura corner near the end, Hearts' heads appeared to drop. Another Nakamura corner was not cleared, but it fell to Stephen McManus whose mis-hit shot was turned into his own goal by keeper Craig Gordon.

It was cruel luck on the Scotland keeper who had turned in a superb performance up to that point.

Falkirk	1	Hearts	1

Hearts were left searching for their first win since October 1 as they were held to a draw by Falkirk who came from behind to snatch a share of the points from the Jambos.

The visitors took the lead on 65 minutes when Velicka squeezed his shot inside the upright when Lambers seemed to have had it covered.

Falkirk showed considerable fight in battling their way back into the game and after a period of pressure on the Hearts goal found an equaliser.

It was Trinidad & Tobago international Russell Latapy, who struck picking up a pass from Alan Gow and stroking the ball past Gordon.

Hearts	0	Rangers	1

A late goal from Nacho Novo gave Rangers a narrow victory at Tynecastle.

The striker's speculative 78th minute shot from outside the box took a deflection to carry it beyond Craig Gordon and into the bottom corner of the net.

Hearts were without Steven Pressley again as Paul Hartley took over the captain's armband.

Andrius Velicka had a chance at the start of the second half but McGregor managed to block the ball and divert it for a corner.

The goal finally arrived with 12 minutes left when Novo was allowed to run unchallenged and he whipped a low shot past Gordon with the aid of a deflection.

Inverness CT	0	Hearts	0

Hearts escaped from the Highland capital with a point after a disappointing goalless draw at Inverness.

The visitors started well and Paul Hartley went close on just two minutes with a dipping drive.

Chances were few and far between, but Barry Wilson forced a fine save from Scotland number one Craig Gordon, then Darren Dods saw his shot deflected wide on 28 minutes.

In the early stages of the second half Hearts took a grip of the game and Takis Fyssas drove a shot over the top on 55 minutes.

The closest Inverness came to breaking through was when Craig Dargo's effort was held after sub Richie Hart sent in a telling cross.

DECEMBER

St Mirren	2	Hearts	2

An end-to-end encounter at Love Street ended 2-2 after a thrilling 90 minutes.

In a sensational start for Hearts, Edgaras Jankauskas sent in a deep cross from the left after only 20 seconds and Saulius Mikoliunas side-footed past Tony Bullock.

Stewart Kean levelled matters crashing a venomous shot past Gordon. Two minutes later, Kean raced on to a Brady pass and slotted an angled drive away from Gordon.

There was no let-up after the interval. Brady, Billy Mehmet and Lappin combined to provide Sutton with a chance but the striker just couldn't connect with the cross. Hearts equalised through a header by Marius Zaliukas.

Hearts	4	Motherwell	1

Bruno Aguiar was the architect of Motherwell's defeat as Hearts registered their first league victory in over two months.

Hearts took the lead after nine minutes when full-back Takis Fyssas ran on to Neil McCann's clever through ball to slip a low finish in off the post.

But Hearts' defensive problems were in evidence as Motherwell hit back quickly through Richie Foran.

Hearts went ahead again through an own-goal from the luckless Paul Quinn as he deflected in Aguiar's effort.

Andrius Velicka raced on to Aguiar's long pass and chipped a delightful finish over Colin Meldrum and Aguiar capped his own excellent performance with a spectacular 25-year free kick.

Hearts	0	Aberdeen	1

A late goal from substitute Steve Lovell lifted Aberdeen into second place in the table ahead of Hearts in a game short of goalmouth action.

Aberdeen almost broke the deadlock early on when Barry Nicholson's corner broke to Russell Anderson. The Dons skipper stabbed a low shot towards the bottom corner but Bruno Aguiar was on the line to clear.

Substitute Paul Hartley gave Hearts a lift when he came on and he had a goal chalked off for offside and then fired a 20-yarder inches wide of the target.

Three minutes from time Scott Severin picked up Jamie Smith's pass and drilled a low 25-yarder that Gordon did well to stop, but Lovell was quickest to react and fired home the loose ball from close range to hand the Dons victory.

Dundee Utd	0	Hearts	1

Christophe Berra took on the role of captain as illness kept Craig Gordon out of the match at Tannadice with Hearts going on to record a one-goal victory.

The home side started strongly but it was Hearts who almost grabbed the lead in the 28th minute when Hartley's free-kick was flicked on by Marius Zaliukas only for a sensational stop from Derek Stillie to prevent the opener.

It was the visitors who grabbed the lead when they were given a penalty by Charlie Richmond in the 53rd minute after Stuart Duff was penalised for handling the ball.

The defender was spotted blocking Panagiotis Fyssas' header and Hartley converted with a well-placed penalty just out Stillie's reach.

Hearts	3	Hibs	2

Hearts edged a breathtaking Edinburgh derby thanks to a late strike from Saulius Mikoliunas at Tynecastle.

Hearts went in front when Roman Bednar pounced on a long through ball and supplied a low cross for Paul Hartley to side-foot the ball home from five yards.

Edgaras Jankauskas was on target three minutes into the second half after an error from Zibi Malkowski.

Hibs were given a lifeline in the 55th minute when Killen powered in a header from Dean Shiels' corner. Shiels then equalised from the penalty spot.

Hearts were back in front after 70 minutes when Mikoliunas cracked in a superb finish from the edge of the box after Hibs were slow to clear their lines.

Kilmarnock	0	Hearts	0

Kilmarnock and Hearts had to settle for a share of the spoils after an exciting encounter at Rugby Park.

After a disappointing first half the match livened up and Hearts shaved both Killie posts within two minutes of the restart as first Mikoliunas volleyed wide before Takis Fyssas burst into the box and shot inches wide.

Killie broke out of their own half in the 55th minute and almost claimed the lead. Allan Johnston slipped the perfect pass to Steven Naismith who chipped over the advancing Craig Gordon but the ball hit the crossbar.

Hearts kept piling the pressure on, and Roman Bednar had an even great chance to win it a minute later from Paul Hartley's beautiful pass, but he blazed over.

MAROON FIVE

Try our unique quiz where every question revolves around the number "5".

 1 Who wore the number five shirt in the season 2006-07?

 2 Which player scored four goals in the 5-1 demolition derby against Hibs at Tynecastle in August 2002?

 3 Who scored Hearts' goals in the 5-1 win over Lokomotiv Leipzig in the European Cup-Winners' Cup in 1976?

 4 Who scored Hearts' goal when they lost 5-1 to Rangers in the 1996 Scottish Cup final at Hampden?

 5 Which Hearts' legend scored five goals in an 8-3 win over Third Lanark at Tynecastle in September 1958?

 6 Hearts opened 1955 with a 5-1 win over which team at Tynecastle?

 7 Who scored Hearts' fifth league goal of last season?

 8 Who was the Number Five who captained the club to the Scottish Cup final win over Celtic in 1956?

 9 How many league appearances did Gary Mackay make for the club – 505, 515 or 525?

10 Which competition did Hearts win in 1985?

11 Donald Ford once scored five goals in an "offside" trial game in the 1960s – who was the opposition?

12 Hearts' first match of 2005 resulted in a 1-1 draw with Hibs at Easter Road – who scored the Hearts' goal?

13 Which player scored twice as Hearts beat Falkirk 5-0 on Boxing Day 2005?

14 Steve Banks had five shut-outs in his six matches for Hearts last season – who were the only team to score past him?

15 Which Estonian team did Hearts beat 5-0 at Tynecastle in the European Cup-Winners' Cup in 1998?

16 Which Hearts' player scored a hat-trick as Hearts ended the 1998-99 season with a handsome 5-2 win over Aberdeen at Pittodrie?

17 When did Hearts first win the Scottish League – 1885, 1895 or 1905?

18 Three players wore the "Number 5" shirt for Hearts during that 1985-86 campaign when Hearts were on the brink of the league title. Roddy MacDonald and Craig Levein were two of them, who was the other?

19 In 1895, Hearts met Hibs for the first time in league competition in front of a record 17,500 crowd at Tynecastle. What was the score?

20 In what year did Hearts turn down a request from Real Madrid to play a challenge match due to fixture congestion – 1925, 1965 or 2005?

Answers on page 61

JANUARY

Dunfermline	0	Hearts	1

Hearts stepped up their challenge for second place with a battling win - their third in four games over the festive period – against the Pars.

Hearts then went ahead when a Bruno Aguiar corner was bundled home at the back post by Czech striker Michal Pospisil - who also scored on his last trip to Fife on the opening day of the season.

As half-time approached Paul Hartley beat the offside trap but could not beat home keeper Roddy McKenzie, while Pospisil crashed a header off the underside of the bar from close range.

Stranraer	0	Hearts	4

An Andrius Velicka hat-trick and a late Roman Bednar strike were enough to help the cup-holders sweep past Stranraer as they began the defence of their CIS Cup crown.

Velicka breezed past Lee Sharp and lobbed home keeper Scott Black as the Jambos got their show on the road in the 17th minute.

Two minutes before the interval Stranraer were hit by the sucker-punch when Velicka headed home after Andy Driver's corner was knocked on into his path by Michal Pospisil.

Substitute Bednar made it three with a powerful 79th minute rising drive and Velicka wrapped up his hat-trick when he squeezed a clever goal home at the post deep into second-half injury-time.

Hearts	1	Celtic	2

Former Hearts skipper Steven Pressley made a victorious return to Tynecastle as his Celtic side came from behind to win 2-1 in front of a packed stadium.

The game sprang into life just before the half-hour mark when a 30-yard wonder strike from Saulius Mikoliunas dipped under the crossbar in the swirling wind and put Hearts into the lead.

Jan Vennegoor of Hesselink was on hand to tap in from inside the six-yard box on the hour mark to equalise for the visitors.

Ten minutes from time, with Celtic continuing to pressure the Hearts goal, Jiri Jarosik found the back of the net for the visitors to snatch victory with a spectacular 20-yard strike.

Hearts	1	Falkirk	0

Substitute Roman Bednar climbed off the bench to fire Hearts to victory with his sixth goal of the season.

The match was played in shocking conditions with strong winds, sleet and snow all making good football virtually impossible.

Kasper Schmeichel showed he is a chip off the old block as he kept Hearts at bay with his string of first-half saves.

But the points were settled in 74 minutes when Bednar reacted quickest to Andrew Driver's cross from the right, to fire a low finish past Schmeichel's despairing dive.

Rangers	0	Hearts	0

In a match where Rangers applied intense pressure after the interval the visitors' defence, well marshalled by Christophe Berra, stood firm as Hearts earned a share of the points at Ibrox.

Rangers skipper Barry Ferguson did have the ball in the net with 13 minutes to go, but was ruled offside.

The Hearts goal had an amazing escape when Charlie Adam headed down to Sionko, who somehow screwed his shot wide from only three yards.

At the start of the second half a free kick from Aguiar went just over before Hearts were pinned back.

FEBRUARY

Dunfermline	1	Hearts	0

Hearts dreams of retaining the Scottish Cup were brought to an abrupt end as they were beaten 1-0 by Dunfermline at East End Park thanks to an injury-time header from skipper Scott Wilson.

He headed in a cross from Adam Hammill just as the match looked like it was heading for a replay.

Dorus de Vries pulled off two excellent saves at the start of the second half to deny firstly Saulius Mikoliunas and then Michal Pospisil.

Roman Bednar came close late on when his chip hit the top of the crossbar, but it was Dunfermline who were to get the goal.

Hearts	1	Inverness CT	0

Michal Pospisil was the Hearts hero as he climbed off the bench to head the winner for Hearts with his very first touch.

Hearts had keeper Steve Banks to thank for a fine early stop when he threw himself to his right, to push away Graham Bayne's close-range volley.

Hearts might have had a penalty when Panagiotis Fyssas went down under Darren Dod's challenge, but it was Banks that kept them level with another fine stop. Barry Wilson was off balance but fired in a 20-yarder that Banks managed to scramble around the post.

But Pospisil had the last laugh when he popped up at the back post to head Andy Driver's cross into the net.

Hearts	1	St Mirren	1

Not for the first time this season, St Mirren took points from their encounter against Hearts.

An early goal from Stephen O'Donnell gave them hope of victory with Hearts all at sea, but a wonder free-kick from Laryea Kingston saved Hearts' blushes.

St Mirren grabbed the opener after 14 minutes when Hearts' central defence went to sleep and Stewart Kean's pass to O'Donnell found him in acres of space as he spun to fire a volley past Craig Gordon from 15 yards.

The Tynecastle side finally found an equaliser and it was a brilliant free-kick from Kingston that he bent over the wall and into the top corner.

MARCH

Motherwell	0	Hearts	2

Hearts cruised to a 2-0 win in difficult conditions at Fir Park as both sides struggled to contend with the swirling rain and greasy surface.

The visitors were eventually rewarded for their enterprise with the opening goal eight minutes before the break as Ibrahim Tall rose unmarked to bullet a header into the net from Laryea Kingston's corner.

The Steelmen should have equalised in the 58th minute when Kingston was forced to clear a Clarkson header off the line.

The visitors grabbed the crucial goal against the run of play in the 66th minute when Well defender Craigan met Kingston's cross and contrived to head the ball past his own keeper at the near post.

Aberdeen	1	Hearts	0

Aberdeen claimed a vital win over nearest rivals Hearts as both teams battled for European qualification.

Aberdeen grabbed the vital opener on eight minutes as Steve Lovell hammered the ball home, giving Craig Gordon no chance.

With the home side now very much in the ascendancy a Russell Anderson flick-on found its way to Brewster, whose volley on the turn was brilliantly palmed away by Gordon.

Hearts day wasn't getting any better when Kingston picked up a red card on 63 minutes for a reckless challenge on Nicholson.

Hearts	0	Dundee Utd	4

Former Hearts boss Craig Levein returned to Tynecastle to steer Dundee United to an emphatic victory.

Hearts, ravaged by injuries, put out a patchwork team and United capitalised as skipper Barry Robson grabbed a glory hat-trick while Lee Wilkie put up the shutters at the back.

Steven Robb charged 40 yards and picked out Robson's run allowing United's captain to fire a low finish past Craig Gordon. Robson ran on to Jon Daly's lay-off and nutmegged Gordon to add United's second on the hour.

Hearts' embarrassment was complete when Hunt got in on the act sliding home Robb's cut-back, before Robson got time and space to cut in off the left and fire in a low drive for United's fourth.

APRIL

Hibs	0	Hearts	1

Marius Zaliukas gave Hearts an unlikely win in the Edinburgh derby to leave Hibs feeling like April Fools at Easter Road.

It was a mistake by goalkeeper Andrew McNeil with just nine minutes left which proved decisive and give Hearts their first derby win at Easter Road for four-and-a-half years.

He failed to deal with a free-kick and slapped the ball into the path of Zaliukas, who accepted the gift.

Craig Gordon had to be at his best to thwart Scott Brown as the home side looked the more likely to open the scoring. But it was Hearts who snatched the win in the closing stages with Zaliukas celebrating his first Edinburgh derby goal.

Hearts	1	Kilmarnock	0

Substitute Michal Pospisil gave Hearts a crucial three points in the quest for a UEFA Cup place with a late strike.

Pospisil headed in a free-kick from Laryea Kingston with just 12 minutes left to settle the issue.

But the game ended in fury as Hearts players reacted angrily to a challenge by Gary Wales on Kingston.

Wales was booked but Goncalves was red carded for his part in the fray that followed in front of the Hearts dugout.

Rangers	2	Hearts	1

Rangers secured a hard-fought victory over Hearts after coming from behind.

Hearts took the lead when Laryea Kingston broke swiftly from midfield before cleverly releasing Andrius Velicka who struck a firm shot into the far corner of the net.

Rangers equalised after a flowing move down the right ended with Alan Hutton intelligently cutting the ball back to Rae who powered an unstoppable header home from ten yards.

Rangers' winner was scored when Brahim Hemdani's header into the penalty area was controlled by Barry Ferguson before he hooked a shot into the top corner.

Celtic	1	Hearts	3

Hearts ruined Celtic's title party with an unexpected 3-1 victory at Celtic Park.

Hearts took the lead in the 57th minute as Laryea Kingston found Kestutis Ivaskevicius with a clever pass and he slid the ball under Artur Boruc.

Celtic were further punished when Andrew Driver curled his free-kick around the wall and into the top corner of the net.

Celtic hit back almost immediately when former Hearts defender Pressley headed home Nakamura's cross from close range.

However, just as the Bhoys were gathering themselves for an onslaught on the Hearts goal, they conceded a penalty which sealed a famous victory for the Jambos.

MAY

Hearts	1	Aberdeen	1

Barry Nicholson kept Aberdeen in control of their UEFA Cup destiny with a dramatic late strike at Tynecastle.

Hearts weathered early Aberdeen pressure but came back to claim the lead after 14 minutes when Zander Diamond needlessly gave up possession and Roman Bednar fed Velicka, who produced a clinical finish under the body of Jamie Langfield.

Hearts came close to a second after an hour when Bednar's shot across goal just eluded substitute Michal Pospisil at the back post.

Nicholson then silenced Tynecastle when he shot the ball past Gordon after being set up by Craig Brewster with just a minute left.

Hearts	2	Hibs	0

Hearts continued to dominate the Edinburgh derby after they beat their old rivals for the third time in a row to move 15 points clear of them in the table.

Any latecomers would have missed the opening goal after barely 30 seconds as Pospisil pounced on a poor clearance and held off Rob Jones and Shelton Martis to find the far corner with his left foot.

Hibs roared back and Steven Fletcher wasted a free header before Driver's deep cross almost found Roman Bednar sliding in at the back post.

Andrew McNeil showed his ability with two excellent saves from Bednar but promptly undid the good work by somehow misjudging a simple catch which allowed Driver to nip in and finish.

Kilmarnock	1	Hearts	0

Steven Naismith's late penalty ended Hearts' hopes of clinching third place SPL and securing European football following a physical contest at Rugby Park.

The Killie youngster calmly slotted home from the spot after being brought down by Craig Gordon to deflate the Jambos, who had enjoyed the bulk of the play.

Hearts produced their best move of the match in the 52nd minute but it ended in Bednar again being denied by a desperate tackle.

Referee Collum pointed to the penalty spot in the 82nd minute when Naismith took advantage of hesitant defending to be brought down by the keeper and he tucked the ball home.

WORD SEARCH

Find these former Hearts' goalkeepers in the word-search.
The words can go vertical, horizontal, diagonal or backwards.

1.	Niemi
2.	Garland
3.	Rousset
4.	Brown
5.	Brough
6.	Walker
7.	Watters
8.	Smith

W	O	K	E	T	S	T	R	U	S	J
F	G	S	P	J	M	G	N	D	R	K
G	A	R	G	T	I	O	W	R	E	P
U	R	A	C	M	T	X	O	I	T	D
E	L	T	E	X	H	U	R	N	T	H
N	A	I	T	T	S	R	B	H	A	C
K	N	F	W	S	O	U	G	L	W	Y
L	D	R	E	K	L	A	W	P	A	B
A	L	T	O	E	H	G	U	O	R	B
W	H	B	R	O	T	Q	S	S	G	D

Answers on page 61

Hearts have been known for their inspired leaders down through the years – players who have led by example and did not pull punches when the chips were down. Here, we look at a few of the great Tynecastle captains who have made significant contributions to the rich history of the club.

Walter Kidd

Walter Kidd spent 14 years at Tynecastle and saw the club move from the first division to jousting with some of the best teams in Europe. He played over 500 games for the club after making his debut in 1977 and never gave less than a hundred per cent. Kidd always led by example and, under Alex MacDonald, played a major role in reviving the club's fortunes in the early 1980s.

He was the first name on MacDonald's teamsheet as his energetic style of tough tackling became a hallmark of Hearts under their new manager.

If he was not noted for his goalscoring exploits (he averaged just a goal a season when he was at the club), his leadership qualities were second to none and he was respected throughout the club and beyond.

His love of the club was best illustrated in that eventful season in 1985-86 when Hearts were on the verge of a league and cup double only for both trophies to be snatched from them in little more than a week.

After the disappointing final day defeat by Dundee in the league, Hearts lost 3-0 to Alex Ferguson's Aberdeen in the Scottish Cup final and Kidd's frustrations boiled over when, earlier having been booked, he was sent off for throwing the ball at Aberdeen's Frank McDougall and thus has the dubious distinction of being the first captain to be sent off in the Scottish Cup final.

He was to continue to play a key role for Hearts but when MacDonald was replaced by Joe Jordan as manager, appearances became more infrequent.

He later went on to join Airdrie where he went on to play in another Scottish Cup final – in 1992 when the Lanarkshire team lost 2-1 to Rangers after beating Hearts in a semi-final replay on penalty kicks.

Gary Locke

Such was the admiration then manager Jim Jefferies had for Gary Locke, he made him Hearts' captain at the age of 20. It is a respect that has grown and Locke was to follow the manager to Bradford and then to Kilmarnock. Locke, who joined the club from Whitehill Welfare, made his mark early and Sandy Clark handed him his Hearts' debut at the age of just 17 in an end-of-season match against St Johnstone in 1993.

Locke impressed to such an extent that he played in the following season's opening game against Rangers at Ibrox and went on to play 39 games that season.

He did not figure as much during Tommy McLean's reign at Tynecastle but, when Jefferies arrived and showed a willingness to give youth a fling, Locke was at the centre of his plans.

A lifelong Hearts' fan, Locke capped a memorable first season under Jefferies when he led the team out in the 1996 Scottish Cup final against Rangers. It was an occasion that was to turn sour after only seven minutes when the player suffered a serious knee injury.

It was an injury that kept him out of the Hearts team that went on to face Rangers in the League Cup final the following season and he made his comeback in January 1997 in a Scottish Cup tie against Cowdenbeath.

As fate would have it, Locke was to miss the 1998 Scottish Cup final against Rangers due to another injury but captain-for-the-day Steve Fulton ensured that he took part in the celebrations as he invited Locke onto the pitch and the pair hoisted the trophy together.

Locke spent almost nine years at Tynecastle before leaving in January 2001 to hook up with Jefferies who was then manager at Bradford.

Dave Mackay

Dave Mackay was regarded as one of the best wing-halves in British football in his time and he gave outstanding service, not only to Hearts, but to Tottenham Hotspur and Derby County.

His time at Tynecastle coincided with one of the most successful periods in the club's history.

Mackay showed his leadership qualities from an early age when he captained Saughton School to the Scottish Schools' Shield when he was 14.

Hearts signed him on an "S" Form and farmed him out to Newtongrange Star where he held his own in the tough world of junior football and it was not long before he was required for first-team duty at Tynecastle.

He made his debut at the age of 18 against Clyde in November 1953 in a 2-1 defeat and, by the following season, he had played no small part in helping Hearts win the League Cup.

He had established himself as a regular in the team by that stage and played in the 4-2 final win over Motherwell and went on to play a total of 36 games for the club that season.

His reputation had grown considerably by the time he played in the Hearts' team that beat Celtic in the 1956 Scottish Cup final at a time when he was doing his national service in England. On the Monday after the final, he had to return to his base south of the border.

Mackay went on to captain Hearts to the league title in 1957-58 – their first title success of the 20th century – and by that stage he was a full Scotland international and attracting interest from some of England's top clubs.

He led Hearts to another League Cup triumph in 1958 but, within a few months, he had signed for Spurs in a £30,000 deal.

He helped the London club win a European trophy in the shape of the Cup-Winners' Cup in 1963 although he missed the final due to a stomach upset.

After a successful spell at Spurs, he joined Derby in 1968 and helped them to the league title under Brian Clough. During his spell at the club, he was voted England's joint Player of the Year with Manchester City captain Tony Book.

Mackay later went on to manage Swindon, Nottingham Forest and Derby.

Tom Purdie

Hearts' first captain – legend has it that Tom Purdie won the honour after a shoot-out with team-mate Jake Reid.

Purdie was a hugely influential figure in Hearts' early days and is even credited with giving the club its name.

A formidable and versatile player, he represented Hearts in defence, at half-back and in attack and his contribution went a long way to establishing the club.

The fierce rivalry with Hibernian helped the club flourish but meetings between the two teams in the early days were plagued by crowd trouble. Purdie was chased by a group of Hibs fans and had to fend them off with a cabbie's whip, according to reports at the time, after he helped Hearts to a 3-2 win in the Edinburgh Association Cup in 1878.

A year later, the player was stoned by Hibs' fans when he was being carried shoulder high by Hearts' supporters after a 1-1 draw between the teams.

He made 50 appearances for the club but had left by the time they won the Scottish Cup for the first time in 1891. He was on the club's committee five years later, however, when the cup was won again.

Summer Signings

Ruben Palazuelos

Hearts beat off competition from clubs around Europe, including Greek giants Panathinaikos, to secure the services of Ruben on a four-year contract signed in July 2007.

Born in Santander, Spain on April 11 2007 Ruben grew up playing in his hometown where he developed into a tough defensive-midfield player. He spent the 2006-07 season at Greek side Aris Thessaloniki making 21 appearances for the club and attracting interest from outside the league. Left-footed Ruben started out in the professional leagues with Spanish Second Division outfit CF Palencia before moving on to Primera Liga side Gimnastic de Tarragona. But he didn't settle into the Tarragona side and was sent out on loan to Thessaloniki.

Since joining up with the club he has impressed in the pre-season friendly against Barcelona. He is expected to form a formidable defensive pairing with Laryea Kingston.

Ricardas Beniusis

Highly rated striker Ricardas joined Hearts in July 2007 on a six-month loan deal from FBK Kaunas. Born in Panevezys, Lituania on April 23 1980 the towering frontman also brings European Champions League experience to the Edinburgh side.

He began his career in 1999 with Inkaras Kaunas scoring 35 goals in 60 appearances for the Lithuanian side.

In 2002 he moved to Atlantas Klaiped making 12 appearances during the season and scoring 6 goals. While there he caught the eye of A Lyga side FBK Kaunas and he signed in July 2003. In the course of his career at FBK he made nearly 100 appearances scoring more than 50 goals for the Lithuanian champions.

The Lithuanian international has been capped 18 times by his country since 2002. His last season at the club proved to be his most prolific netting 16 goals in 15 A Lyga matches.

Audrius Ksanavicius

Lithuanian Audrius came to Hearts on a six-month loan deal from FBK Kaunas.

The highly rated midfielder has won eight senior caps for his country and brings a wealth of experience with him to Tynecastle.

Born on January 28, 1977 he attracted a great deal of attention early on in his career earning caps at youth and Under-21 level for his country. The left-sided player who began his professional career at FBK in 1994 played against Scotland in an Under-21 match in 1999 scoring one of the goals on the way to a 2-1 victory for Lithuania.

In 2002 he joined Skonto Riga playing 36 matches and scoring nine goals for the Latvian Virsliga champions before moving back to FBK Kaunas in 2004 but spent 2005 on loan with Atlantas Klaipeda.

Michael Stewart

An Edinburgh lad through and through, midfielder Michael made history in June 2007 becoming the first player since World War 2 to move directly from Hearts to Hibs then back again.

Born in Edinburgh on February 26 1981 Michael grew up supporting Hearts as he attended Craigmount High School. But his football career began at Rangers where he came through the youth system before signing with Manchester Utd in March 1998. He made his senior debut for the Red Devils against Watford in October 2000 While impressing in England Michael also caught the attention of the national side and after several appearances with the Under-21 side he was called up by Scotland manager Berti Vogts earning three caps for his country in 2002.

After spending a season on loan at Nottingham Forest in 2003/04 Michael returned north to join Hearts in a season-long loan deal. Unfortunately an injury-hit season meant that he only played 13 league games before moving on to Edinburgh rivals Hibs in 2005. On June 30 2007, he signed for Hearts.

MICHAEL STEWART
ACROSS THE GREAT

There is a select band of players who have worn both the maroon of Hearts and the green of Hibs. Players such as Gordon Smith, Alan Gordon, Andy Watson, Darren Jackson and Paul Hartley have all been toasted – and heckled - by both sides of Edinburgh at different stages of their careers.

But, last summer, MICHAEL STEWART made history by signing for Hearts from Hibs – just two years after leaving Tynecastle for Hearts' greatest rivals - in a unique double switch directly between the clubs.

The midfield player is a fervent Scottish nationalist and here he outlines why he thinks Scottish football is important to the nation's wellbeing.

Michael Stewart wants Scottish football to come in from the cold. Having spent six years at Manchester United and enjoyed the best training facilities the game can offer, he knows that not every team has access to such luxury.

Hearts had the foresight to build a training academy at Riccarton and Rangers, Celtic and now Hibs have invested heavily in their own custom-built facilities as Scotland finally drags itself into the 21st century.

"I look at England where there is more money in the clubs and I'd say nine out of ten big clubs down there have their own facilities," Stewart points out."

"If we're talking about improving the national team, we can't just look at the top tier of the game."

"You need to look at the grass-roots and getting youngsters involved in the sport. If you ask a kid to go out and train in the pouring rain when the facilities are poor, there is no danger they'll be looking forward to it."

"Whereas if we had two or three facilities in Edinburgh and two or three in Glasgow and right throughout the country – in Dundee and Aberdeen and Inverness – then you start to have a basis to progress and in future, you'll improve the national team."

Stewart is calling on the Scottish Executive to provide the funds to build such facilities.

DIVIDE

"I know it's difficult because there are a million and one things that need extra funding but I think that football is such an important part of the psyche of the country," he continued.

"For too long now, we've neglected it in terms of funding. If you look at other countries throughout Europe, they're bearing fruit now in terms of what they're producing because of the funding that's been put into them."

"Elsewhere, if you look at Australia, across the board sports wise they are picking up golds at the Olympics right, left and centre because of the Sports Institute system."

"It doesn't mean that we should throw our hands up and say we're 30 years behind, we need to put it in place now. There's no point in putting it off any longer."

"The money that football generates for the economy should be put back into it. It is such a high priority in this country and produces such a feel-good factor for us."

"I also think that Scotland should try and go for a major tournament and it should have the full backing of the government and not any wishy-washy support."

"If you look at every country that hosts a major tournament, not only do they get a feel-good factor but they get the economic benefit afterwards."

Not many Scottish footballers see "Newsnight" as an essential part of their television viewing but Stewart has a keen interest in politics and might even consider it as a possible career when he hangs up his boots.

"I really don't know if I'd ever consider going into politics. It's something that interests me and I've developed it over the years," he states.

"I'm at the stage now, where I take a deep interest in the politics that are going on at the moment. But in terms of going into politics, it's something that's off in the distance at the moment and whether I could make any difference, I don't know."

For now, Stewart will concentrate on making his mark for Hearts on the football field and attempting to prove to Hibs they were wrong to let him go.

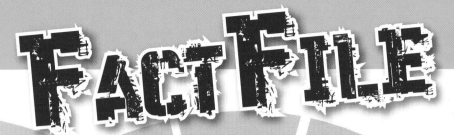

20 Essential Facts About Your Favourite Club

Hearts held a raffle to help pay for a new wooden grandstand at the club in 1901 which was erected at the cost of £647.00.

Hibs played home matches at Tynecastle in the 1924-25 season when they were constructing a new stand at Easter Road.

Legendary player Bobby Walker received a national testimonial for his services to the game and was given 250 gold sovereigns and a pocket watch.

The first half-time scoreboard was erected at Tynecastle in 1908 by the Exchange Telegraph Company who also issued the first regular programme for matches.

When Scotland drew 1-1 with England in 1907 there were only two home-based players in the team – both from Hearts (Bobby Walker and Charlie Thomson).

Jimmy Murray is the only Hearts' player to have scored for Scotland during a World Cup finals – against Yugoslavia in Sweden in 1958.

Peter Fairley was the first manager of the club and held the post from April 1901 to August 1903.

John McCartney was replaced as manager of the club in November 1991 – by his son William, who was a referee!

Former Arsenal and England goalkeeper Frank Moss was the first manager to have full powers of team selection when he took over in 1937, having retired from playing at the age of 28 due to injury.

Hearts once faced Rangers – back in the 1925-26 season – in a golf match at Gleneagles.

David Russell was the first Hearts' player to score a league hat-trick – achieving the feat in a 4-3 win over Renton in September 1891.

The Tynecastle pitch used to face east-west but was moved to its current north-south setting in 1888.

Willie Mackay has the distinction of scoring Hearts' only ever goal in the English FA Cup. He netted in a 7-1 defeat by Darwen in Lancashire in 1886.

Rangers were Hearts' first opponents in the Scottish League in August 1890. Hearts lost 5-2 at Ibrox.

Celtic were Hearts' first league opponents at Tynecastle – a week after the opener against Rangers – and the Glasgow side returned west with a 5-0 win to celebrate.

Hearts have only once failed to fulfil a league fixture. At the end of the 1915-16 season, the club did not play a fixture against Morton at Cappielow due to shortage of players and wartime travel problems. The result would not have changed the league positions and Hearts escaped punishment.

Isaac Begbie captained Hearts to their first league title in 1894-95 in a season where they lost only two league games – both to Clyde.

Otto Jonsson, an Icelandic amateur player, became the first foreigner to play for Hearts back in the 1944-45 season.

When Hearts beat Hibs 2-1 at Easter Road on January 2, 1950 it was in front of the biggest crowd to watch a match in Scotland outside of Glasgow with 65,840 packing the stadium.

Willie Ormond and Willie McCartney share the distinction of being the only managers to have taken charge at both Hearts and Hibs.

Hearts made their Champions League debut last season and got off to a flier. But, ultimately, the dream of reaching the group stages was ended by a slick AEK Athens team. But there was still the consolation of playing in the UEFA Cup - here we look back at Hearts' last European campaign.

Champions League: Second Qualifying round: First leg: Hearts 3 Siroki Brijeg 0

The euphoria of Paul Hartley's spot-kick against Aberdeen at the end of the previous season which clinched Champions League qualification was still evident as a crowd of 28,486 - Hearts' biggest in Europe for 46 years - turned up at Murrayfield.

The fact that the game was being played before the end of July meant that both sides looked a little rusty in the first half but it was Hearts who all but booked their place in the next qualifying round with a late flourish.

The Edinburgh side started in positive fashion and Neil McCann, back in maroon for the first time in almost eight years, came close with one early header.

The Bosnian team had their chances too in an untidy first half with Brazilian Wagner going close on a couple of occasions.

But it was Hearts who made the breakthrough eight minutes into the second half. A long throw-in from Robbie Neilson put Branimir Anic in trouble and, under pressure from Steven Pressley, he headed the ball into his own net for Hearts' first goal in the Champions League.

The game was more open after the goal and Deividas Cesnauskis went close with a shot which skipped just wide of the post before a Bruno Aguiar free-kick struck the crossbar.

The crucial second goal came with 12 minutes left when Ibrahim Tall, after initially making a mess of a cutback from Michal Pospisil, recovered his composure to drill the ball home.

It became even better for Hearts six minutes later when Roman Bednar took advantage of some slack defending to slip home the third goal and send the Hearts' fans home happy.

Champions League: Second Qualifying round: Second leg: Siroki Brijeg 0 Hearts 0

Hearts returned a disciplined away performance in Europe to stifle Siroki and book a final qualifying round place against AEK Athens.

Protecting a three-goal lead from the first leg, Hearts rarely looked in trouble and moved through comfortably. Valdas Ivanauskas' side started well and Siroki goalkeeper Vladimir Vasilj failed to hold a free-kick from Roman Bednar but recovered in time to prevent Christophe Berra from pouncing on the rebound.

Vasilj had a lucky escape when he palmed a Neil McCann corner into his own net but the Hungarian referee spotted a Hearts player pushing in the penalty area and disallowed the "goal".

Siroki finally threatened after 16 minutes when Mislav Karoglen brought the save of the match from Craig Gordon with a left-foot shot from 25 yards which swerved wickedly.

Gordon excelled again midway through the first half after a well-worked free-kick with Karoglen again having the final shot.

Karoglen was proving the main dangerman but Hearts were well organised at the back and Siroki's best efforts were from distance.

A minute from the break, Gomes completely missed the ball ten yards out after a fluent move and when the ball broke to Josip Papic, he sent his 18-yard shot well over the top.

Hearts had another escape early in the second half when Wagner cut the ball back to Celson but his shot was brilliantly blocked by Gordon.

Hearts responded and McCann was not far away from connecting with a fiercely-struck Bednar cross at the back post but the match was to finish goalless.

Champions League: Third Qualifying round: First leg: Hearts 1 AEK Athens 2

Hearts' hopes of progressing to the group stages of the Champions League were left hanging by a thread as they lost to a slick AEK Athens at Murrayfield in a dramatic finish.

Pantelis Kapetonas headed an 89th minute equaliser after 10-man Hearts looked like stealing an unlikely win and then Nikos Liberopoulos scored in injury time with a

shot which deflected off Christophe Berra to leave Craig Gordon helpless.

Hearts struggled for long periods but a 62nd minute goal from Saulius Mikoliunas gave them the lead before Bruno Aguiar was sent off four minutes later after picking up two bookings.

Watched by a crowd of 32,459, there was a let-off for the home side after only three minutes when Steven Pressley headed a Julio Cesar corner against his own crossbar. Liberopoulos then came close with a shot from just outside the area which was just a yard too high.

But Hearts responded and a left-foot shot from Mikoliunas took a deflection and hit the outside of the post with Stefano Sorrentino beaten.

Takis Fyssas then raced clear on the left and his cross found Mikoliunas but the Lithuanian rushed his effort and it finished well over the top.

Liberopoulos showed his menace again when he cracked in a 19-yard shot which bounced in front of Gordon but skipped wide.

AEK came close again nine minutes from the break when Michal Pospisil headed against the outside of his own post from another Julio Cesar corner.

A fingertip save from Gordon then denied the quick-thinking Julio Cesar after Pressley had given the ball away.

Aguiar had a chance after 59 minutes but Mikoliunas obstructed him and he could only hook the ball wide. Mikoliunas made amends when he scored three minutes later when he shot home from six yards after a Roman Bednar shot had come off the post.

Hearts were reduced to ten men after 66 minutes when Aguiar picked up his second booking for preventing AEK taking a quick free-kick.

Hearts were on the ropes in the closing minutes and Kapetonas finally scored with a header before Liberopoulos hit the winner with a shot which spun off Christophe Berra.

Champions League: Third Qualifying round: Second leg: AEK Athens 3 Hearts 0

Hearts were left with mission impossible in Athens as they ended this match with just nine players.

Julien Brellier was bizarrely sent off in the 29th minute after picking up two yellow cards in the space of five minutes.

He was booked for coming onto the field without permission after receiving treatment and then yellow carded again for challenging for the ball with his arm raised.

Neil McCann was then sent off after 63 minutes for a two-footed challenge on Vladimir Ivic.

Late goals from Julio Cesar (2) and Nikos Liberopoulos settled a controversial match, which saw a total of eight bookings.

Valdas Ivanauskas sprang a surprise before kick-off when he started with teenage striker Jamie Mole, who was yet to start an SPL match.

AEK started strongly and Liberopoulos was only a yard too high with a shot before Pantelis Kapetanos missed the target with a free header from six yards.

Hearts hit back and Paul Hartley missed the easiest of opportunities when he headed straight at Dionisios Chiotis after a great flick from McCann.

AEK also had their chances and Panagiotis Lagos shot straight at Craig Gordon when he was clean through and Liberopoulos somehow sent a header wide from just three yards.

It was backs-to-the-wall stuff in the second half for Hearts but, for all their possession, AEK did not show too much adventure in front of goal.

Four minutes after McCann was sent off Liberopoulos had another shooting chance, but it was a comfortable save for Gordon.

The breakthrough eventually came when Deividas Cesnauskis fouled Vasilis Lakis in the penalty box in the 79th minute and Julio Cesar fired the spot-kick high into the net.

Liberopoulos then made it 2-0 with a head-flick from ten yards, before Julio Cesar took advantage of slack play from Edgaras Jankauskas to lash home the third from 16 yards.

UEFA Cup: First round: First leg: Hearts 0 Sparta Prague 2

Hearts were left with a mountain to climb to maintain interest in the UEFA Cup as they lost to a well-drilled Sparta side at Murrayfield.

Substitute Miroslav Matusovic scored a late goal to add to Daniel Kolar's first-half opener to all but make the second leg in the Czech Republic a formality.

Hearts were hit by injuries and suspensions and Mirsad Beslija came into the midfield

and Jamie Mole was also included.

Sparta looked more dangerous throughout and Ludovic Sylvestre slid a shot narrowly wide early on after exchanging passes with Libor Dosek.

Karol Kisel then shot wildly over the top after another dangerous Czech move had Hearts on the back foot.

Craig Gordon was the busier of the two goalkeepers and he did brilliantly to touch a shot from Sylvestre over the bar for a corner.

It was no surprise when Kolar beat the Scotland goalkeeper with a well-placed right-foot shot from the edge of the box which flew high into the net after 33 minutes.

Hearts were in further trouble when Jiri Homola had a header from just two yards out from a Jan Simak corner but sent his effort over the crossbar when he should have scored.

The home side had a chance to equalize moments before half-time but Mauricio Pinilla sent his header straight into the arms of Jaromir Blazek from a Paul Hartley corner.

Hearts started the second half better and Mole was denied by Blazek after 58 minutes after working himself an opportunity.

But Sparta were always dangerous on the break and substitute Matusovic should have done better with an effort from six yards out which he sent wide.

Gordon made superb stops in quick succession from Libor Dosek and then Kisel to keep Hearts hanging on. But the goal was only delayed until the 71st minute when Matusovic took a pass from Kisel and fired a low shot into the corner of the net to kill off the home side.

UEFA Cup: First round: Second leg: Sparta Prague 0 Hearts 0

Hearts paid the price for a dismal first leg performance as they bowed out of the UEFA Cup in spite of a notable result in Prague.

After weathering a first-half storm, Hearts had their chances to retrieve the tie but could not muster enough to seriously concern the home side.

The Edinburgh side were under the cosh from the early moments and Paul Hartley reacted well to hook a close-in header from Libor Dosek off the line.

Jan Simek then shot just a foot wide from 25 yards with the Hearts' defence guilty of giving him too much space. Mauricio Pinilla had Hearts' only first-half effort on target with an early header which Jaromir Blazek dealt with expertly.

But there was a let off for Hearts in the 13th minute when Daniel Kolar's shot took a deflection and thumped against the crossbar with Craig Gordon beaten.

There was another narrow escape after 29 minutes when Tomas Sivok had a free header at a corner, but sent his effort wide when he should have done better.

The home side were well in control, but Hearts improved towards half-time and a mistake by goalkeeper Blazek gave Jamie Mole an opening but the angle was too tight and he failed to take advantage.

Deividas Cesnauskis wasted a good chance to put Hearts in front six minutes from the break when he volleyed high and wide with his left foot when he had a chance at the back post.

Cesnauskis had a better effort a minute from half-time when he guided a shot narrowly wide after Sparta failed to clear a Hartley free-kick.

Mole missed the best chance after 48 minutes when he only had Blazek to beat but he shot straight at the goalkeeper and he diverted it for a corner.

If anything, Hearts looked the more likely to break the deadlock in the second half as Sparta seemed content to sit on their first-leg advantage.

Hearts just could not step it up enough in the final stages to salvage the tie, although substitute Roman Bednar went close in injury-time.

A-Z CHRISTOPHE BERRA

A is for April – Christophe signed his first professional contract with the club in April 2002.

B is for Bank of Scotland Young Player of the Month – He picked up the award in January 2007 after impressing with his consistency.

C is for Champions League – Christophe had an early taste in his career with the matches against Siroki Brijeg and AEK Athens.

D is for Didier – Christophe's middle name, reflecting his dad's French roots.

E is for Edina Hibs – Christophe learned his trade at the club before signing professional forms for Hearts in 2002.

F is for France – Through his father's lineage, Christophe could have played for France.

G is for Gordon – Christophe quickly worked out an understanding with Craig Gordon which has kept the defence solid.

H is for Hearts' Young Player of the Year – At the end of season awards dinner last May, he was voted the club's young player for the 2006-07 season.

I is for Italy – Christophe gained his first Scotland Under-21 cap in a 2-0 defeat by Italy in Pavia.

J is for January – It's birthday month for Christophe and in January 2008, he will celebrate his 23rd birthday on the 31st!

K is for Kilmarnock – The defender netted his first goal for the club when he scored the second goal in a 2-0 win over Kilmarnock in April, 2006, to clinch the victory.

L is for Levein – It was Craig Levein who signed Christophe for Hearts and spotted his potential to go all the way to the top.

M is for Motivator – The central defender has had to make himself heard on the pitch and has shown his leadership qualities.

N is for Nostalgia – Christophe went to secondary school just a stone's throw from The Meadows, where Hearts first played their home games.

O is for Osasuna – The Spanish side were at Murrayfield for a pre-season friendly in 2006 and little did Christophe know after Hearts' 2-0 win that Osasuna would go on to reach the last four of the UEFA Cup before losing to eventual winner Seville.

P is for Pace – Christophe has been blessed with electric pace which has helped him match the quickest strikers in the Scottish game.

Q is for Queen's Park – Was in the Hearts team that played at Hampden in the League Cup tie in August 2005, but was unfortunate to miss the Scottish Cup final at the same venue at the end of that season.

R is for Regular – Christophe established himself as a regular in the Hearts' team in 2006-07.

S is for St Thomas of Aquin's High School – Christophe attended the Edinburgh school where he first harboured thoughts of a full-time career in the game.

T is for Tannadice – It was at the home of Dundee United that Christophe made his competitive debut for the club, coming on for Neil MacFarlane in a 2-1 defeat in November 2003.

A-Z CHRISTOPHE BERRA

U is for Understudy – Christophe had to bide his time under Steven Pressley and Andy Webster and covered for injuries and suspensions in his first couple of seasons.

V is for Valdas – Ivanauskas rated Christophe highly when he was in charge and tipped him for a full Scotland call-up.

W is for Webster – Christophe learned a lot from working closely with Andy Webster at the club.

X is for x-rated – Christophe was desperately unlucky to see a shot deflect off him in injury-time in the Champions League tie with AEK Athens at Murrayfield to give the Greeks victory.

Y is for Yellow Cards – After picking up three in the final five matches of last season, Christophe missed the opening of this season's SPL campaign.

Z is for Zaliukas – Not a partnership Hearts fans would have anticipated in central defence at the start of last season but it worked brilliantly.

Juho Makela

The Finnish striker is hoping for a big season after spending the second half of last season on loan at Swiss side TC Thun.

After scoring a hat-trick in his first start for Hearts – against Alloa in the CIS Cup – he scored his first Premier League goal in the 4-0 win over Dundee United at Tynecastle in October, 2006.

His treble against Alloa is remembered as the perfect hat-trick – one with each foot and a header.

But he only made 11 appearances last season and was allowed to go out on loan and his time in Switzerland, most spent battling against relegation, proved the perfect tonic.

He returned to Hearts and scored against Barcelona in the pre-season friendly at Murrayfield and wants to make himself a regular fixture in the Hearts' team.

Born in Oulu, he started out with his local team OLS Oulu but earned his big break when he moved to HJK Helsinki in 2003.

Spent three seasons with the club where he netted 33 goals in 66 appearances and, after representing Finland at Under-21 level, won his first full international cap for his country against China in February, 2004.

Moved to Hearts in January 2006 during the transfer window where he signed a three-and-a-half-year contract.

Noted for his pace, the club is hoping that 2007-08 will be his big breakthrough year in Scotland.

Robbie Nielson

Tynecastle stalwart Robbie confirmed his position as one of Scotland's most reliable defenders when he was awarded his first Scotland cap at the start of the 2006/07 season.

The longest-serving Hearts player turned out for the national team in the 2-0 defeat to Ukraine in October 2007.

Born on June 19, 1980, the dependable right-back signed from Rangers Boys Club but took several years to establish himself as a first-team regular at Tynecastle. He was in the Hearts' youth team that won the BP Youth Cup in 1998 and, after gaining youth caps for Scotland, was called up for the Scotland Under-21 squad in spite of the fact he had not yet played first-team football for Hearts.

After playing in all but one of Hearts' league matches in the 2005-06 season Robbie has struggled with injury in 2007 but still managed to register 23 appearance for the Edinburgh side to take his tally of first-team matches played for the club to 166.

Ibrahim Tall

Ibrahim made a real breakthrough into the Hearts side in 2006/07 establishing himself as a first-team regular and an integral part of the Tynecastle defence.

The Senegalese international joined the club in August 2005 from FC Sochaux-Montbeliard but his appearances were limited until the past season when he had 29 outings in a Hearts shirt.

Born on June 23 1981, Ibrahim is a tall defender who is equally comfortable at right-back or in the centre of defence but it took until the final weeks of the 2005/06 season for him to break into the Hearts side under manager Valdas Ivanauskas.

He began his professional career in France with CS Louhans-Cuiesaux before moving up the leagues.

A regular in the Sochaux team for three seasons, Ibrahim made over 70 appearances for the club as well as picking up international caps for Senegal.

The 2006/07 season saw Ibrahim get his name on the scoresheet for the first time since moving to Edinburgh as he netted his first goal in Hearts' European Cup match against NK Siroki in July 2006. He scored again in the 2-0 SPL win over Motherwell in March 2007.

Having made the successful breakthrough to the first-team Ibrahim is expected to continue in the core of the Hearts defence for sometime to come.

Neil McCann

Veteran midfielder Neil has bounced back from a serious knee injury that ended his 2005/06 season to re-establish himself as the reliable player that Hearts can call in midfield.

In his second spell with Hearts after re-signing from Southampton in January 2006, Neil made 28 appearances in a Hearts shirt in 2006/07 to take his tally of matches for the club to over 100.

Born in Greenock on November 8 1974 Neil started his career at Dundee before moving on to Hearts in 1996 and then Rangers two years later.

He was one of the Hearts heroes who beat Rangers 2-1 in the 1998 Scottish Cup Final to lift the trophy but missed out on the 2006 victory over Gretna due to injury.

He joined Southampton on August 5 2003 for £1.5million but a series of injuries made it difficult for him to maintain his place in the team and he decided on a return to Scotland.

Neil has made nearly 30 appearances for the Scottish national side, his debut coming in September 1998 against Lithuania.

Michal Pospisil

The big Czech striker has continued to prove that he can score goals at crucial times for Hearts despite suffering an injury disrupted season in 2006/07

After picking up an injury in mid-August 2006 Michal missed nearly four months of action on the sidelines recovering which makes his tally of six goals during the season even more impressive.

He marked his return to form with a goal in the SPL win over Dunfermline at East End Park in early January.

Michal signalled his commitment to the club after turning his back on a move to Bristol City midway through the season and continues to be an important member of the first team.

Born on May 3 1979 Michal is a strong, aggressive forward, at 6'3" he poses a major aerial threat, particularly at set-pieces.

Michal joined the club in July 2005 from Slovan Liberec where he has built up a reputation as one of the Czech Republic's most exciting strikers.

Michal was part of the Czech side which won the European U21 Championships in 2002. He contributed the first penalty for his country as they beat France in the final shoot-out.

He played in the Champions League with Sparta before moving on to Viktoria Zizkov where he played in the UEFA Cup and won the Czech Republic Cup and has since gone on to play for Hearts in their European campaigns.

Roman Bednar

Roman began the 2006/07 season in formidable form scoring four goals in his first four appearances on the season.

As well as being an invaluable asset to Hearts this also earned him his first senior cap for his home nation, the Czech Republic in their match against Serbia in August 2006.

A formidable presence in the box, powerful striker Roman Bednar attracted interest from clubs around Europe since his time with Czech Second Division side FK Mlada Boleslav in 2004 until he was brought to Hearts by George Burley in the summer of 2005.

Born on March 26 1983 Roman began his career at CAFC Prague in his native Czech Republic before moving to the Czech First Division in 1998 with Bohemians Prague but he has since gone on to become a firm favourite with the Tynecastle faithful having scored 13 times in the short time he has been at the club.

Roman is one year into a four-year contract with the Edinburgh side and fans will be looking for many more goals from the man who was once voted 'Discovery of the Year' in the Czech league.

Saulius Mikoliunas

Saulius earned himself legendary status with the Hearts faithful on Boxing Day 2006 as he scored the winner in the Edinburgh Derby. With 20 minutes remaining the old rivals were locked at 2-2 but the Lithuanian international stepped up to give Hearts a famous victory.

Born on May 2 1984 Saulius made an immediate impact on Scottish football and has continued to impress for Hearts scoring five goals last season.

He started out at Lithuanian club Sviesa Vilnius before joining FBK Kaunas in 2003. He gained a reputation as one of the country's most dangerous front men when FBK won the Lithuanian Championship in 2004.

He has become a regular in the Lithuanian international side and featured in the Champions League with FBK.

The Lithuanian international proved himself a quick and skilful winger in his debut against Livingston on January 25 2005 and scored his first goal for the club in the 3-0 win over Kilmarnock on February 12.

Steve Banks

Steve continues to provide reliable back-up for Craig Gordon at the same time as proving he has all the credentials to be a top class goalkeeper having conceded just one goal in the six matches he played in the 2006/07 season.

Despite only making nine appearances since joining the club in August 2005, Steve is highly regarded at Tynecastle and the club are delighted that the Englishman has signed on for another season in Edinburgh

Born on September 9 1972, Steve started his career at West Ham in 1990 as a trainee but after failing to break through into the first team he moved to Gillingham, a club he later returned to before his move to Scotland.

After two seasons and nearly 70 appearances for The Gills he moved to Blackpool where he played over 180 matches in just under 4 years.

Moves to Bolton, Rochdale, Bradford, Stoke City and Wimbledon followed before his return to Gillingham in March 2004.

Christophe Berra

One of the most successful products of the Hearts youth system, home-town boy Christophe is now the heart of the Tynecastle defence.

Born on January 31, 1985, Christophe signed professional forms in April 2002 after impressing in the youth side.

Considered a developing player in previous seasons and given limited first-team exposure Christophe has blossomed into a top-team regular in the 2006/07 season making 44 appearances for the club.

Although he is eligible to play for France thanks to his father's nationality, Christophe has decided to represent Scotland and has played up to Under-21 level with a full international career surely just around the corner.

Having signed a long-term contract with the club in July 2006, Christophe is expected to become a true Hearts great in years to come.

Deividas Cesnauskis

Deividas made an immediate impact on Hearts club as he scored on his debut in the Scottish Cup Fourth Round replay against Kilmarnock on February 16 2005 and he has remained firmly in the first-team picture since that time.

Despite failing to find the back of the net in the 2006/07 season the Lithuanian midfielder made 14 appearances for the Edinburgh side as well as continuing to star in the Lituanian national team.

He has earned over 20 caps for his country and started his playing days at FK Ekranas Panevezys playing in the Lithuanian Cup Final win in May 2000. He rapidly attracted attention from outside his home country and was signed up by Dynamo Moscow in 2001. He moved across the Russian capital in December 2003 to join Lokomotiv Moscow and helped them to the Russian League Championship.

Born on June 30 1981 Deividas was on his way back to his Lithuanian roots and FBK Kaunas when Hearts swooped in to sign him, beating off strong opposition for his services from other European sides.

Deividas has a younger brother Edgaras who is also a professional footballer and currently plays for Saturn Ramenskoe in Russia.

PLAYER PROFILES

Calum Elliot

Youngster Calum grew in stature in the 2007/08 season after spending the first half out on loan at Motherwell.

Having made 17 appearances for the Fir Park side, including two goals, the skilful attacker returned to Tynecastle and was immediately pulled into first-team action against Dunfermline in January 2007 and he went on to make nine first-team appearances.

Born in Edinburgh on March 30 1987 teenager Calum is a product of the Hearts Youth set-up who has fought his way into the first team on the back of solid performances which belie his young age.

He was handed his senior debut in September 2004 against Inverness Caledonian Thistle but only went on to make a handful of appearances in his first full season.

2005/06 proved to be the breakthrough season for the striker as he made 34 first-team appearances and scored six goals including a double in the SPL match against Falkirk on Boxing Day.

Jose Goncalves

Jose has overcome an injury-plagued first season at Hearts to become a first-team regular at the club making 12 appearances for the Tynecastle side in 2006/07.

Defender Jose was born in Portugal on September 17 1985 but raised in Switzerland where he moved at the age of two with his parents. He began playing football at FC Basel where he came through the youth set up and got his professional debut in 2004 when he was signed up by Swiss Challenge League club FC Winterthur.

In January 2005 Jose moved to Italian Serie B club AC Venezia but made just three appearances but months later returned to Switzerland where he was signed by FC Thun.

While at Thun he played in the Champions League eight times including matches against European giants such as Arsenal and Ajax.

He made his Hearts debut on February 4 2006 in the 3-0 win over Aberdeen at Tynecastle and went on to make six league and cup appearances in his first season.

Christos Karipidis

After signing from Greek side PAOK Salonika in August 2006 Christos has enjoyed a successful first season with Hearts making 16 first-team appearances.

The defender Christos came up through the youth system at PAOK and got his break for the club in 2001 before a brief spell on loan to AO Kavala later that year and a second period away at AO Kerkyre in 2003.

Born on December 2 1982 in Thessaloniki, Christos went on to be part of the PAOK's UEFA Cup squad in 2004 and again in 2005 when he lined up against Shakhtar Donetsk, VfB Stuttgart and Rapid Bucharest. He added to his European CV as he turned out for Hearts against AEK Athens in August 2006.

Christos has also played on the international stage featuring in the football tournament at the Olympic Games in Athens in 2004 for Greece.

Lee Wallace

Following his first-team breakthrough in 2005 Edinburgh-born Lee has gone on to establish himself as a firm favourite at Tynecastle making 23 first-team appearances in 2006/07.

Alongside team-mate Calum Elliot, Wallace was an integral part of the Scotland U-19 team that reached the final of the 2006 UEFA U/19 Championships before narrowly losing to Spain. He started every match at left back.

He made his playing debut in the Scottish Cup Fourth Round draw against Kilmarnock on February 5 2005. Before going on to impress team mates and fans by running 70 yards to score a stunning individual goal in the replay ten days later setting Hearts on the road to victory.

Born on August 21 1987 the left-back has found his niche on the left side of the defence forcing more experienced players out of the position.

Possessing an old head on young shoulders he has drawn comparisons with former Hearts defender and Scotland regular Gary Naysmith.

Laryea Kingston

Midfielder Laryea has made an immediate impact on Hearts since arriving in January 2007 making 11 first team appearances and scoring one goal in his first few months at the club.

The Ghana international, born in Accra on November 7 1980, signed on loan from Lokamotiv Moscow but has since committed himself to Hearts signing on for another season as a Tynecastle player.

He made his debut on February 2 2007 in the Scottish Cup fourth-round defeat against Dunfermline at East End Park and his first goal came two weeks later as his strike earned Hearts a share of the points as they came from behind to draw with St Mirren.

Laryea started his career with his local side Great Olympics, whom he joined aged 16, before moving to Libyan side Al-Ittihad in 2000, on a loan deal. However, after only 4 months of this arrangement he returned to Accra joining one of Ghana's traditional "Big Two", Hearts of Oak, in 2001.

Two years later he moved to Israel, initially with Maccabi Ahi Nazareth. After two Toto Cup matches, Maccabi decided not to retain him and he was signed by Hapoel Tel Aviv, where he played until 2004.

Andrew Driver

Hearts made sure to sign Englishman Andrew Driver on a long-term contract which should see him at the club until 2011 after he impressed in his first full season in the Tynecastle first team.

Born on November 12 1987 in Oldham, Driver moved to Edinburgh as a teenager and came up through the Hearts youth system.

He first made his mark on Hearts' first team during a pre-season tour of Austria in 2006, where he started all 3 friendlies, creating four goals in the process with his direct play and crossing ability.

He made a dream home debut in the league on 26 August 2006 against Inverness Caledonian Thistle, coming on as a substitute with 15 minutes to go and scoring four minutes later.

In December 2006 he made his first competitive start for the club in the 1-0 win over Dundee Utd at Tannadice. He later scored memorable goals against Celtic at Celtic Park and Hibs in the Edinburgh derby.

euroquiz

Hearts have enjoyed many memorable nights in Europe. Test your knowledge as we take a trip down memory lane.

1 Who scored Hearts' first goal in European competition?

2 Which team did Hearts record their first victory against in Europe?

3 Who were the first team Hearts knocked out of Europe?

4 Which German team knocked Hearts out of the Cup-Winners' Cup in 1976?

5 Who scored Hearts' first UEFA Cup goal?

6 Which Czech Republic team put Hearts out of the 1986-87 UEFA Cup on the away goals rule?

7 Which player scored in five of Hearts' eight ties during their memorable run in the 1988-89 UEFA Cup?

8 Which Italian team ended Hearts' interest in Europe in 1990-91?

9 Which former Everton player scored a memorable European goal against Slavia Prague at Tynecastle in 1992?

10 Which Dutch legend was manager of FC Liege when they played Hearts in the 1992-93 UEFA Cup?

11 Who scored Hearts' goals when they beat Atletico Madrid 2-1 in the first round of the 1993-94 UEFA Cup?

12 Steve Frail has played in only one European match for Hearts – who were the opponents?

13 Who were Hearts' scorers in the thrilling 3-2 win over Stuttgart at Tynecastle in September, 2000?

14 Who scored the only goal against Bordeaux in 2003 when Hearts gained one of their best European results away from home?

15 What was significant about Hearts' 2-2 draw with SC Braga in Portugal in September 2004?

16 Which player notched his first goal for the club to give Hearts a dramatic 2-1 win over FC Basle in Switzerland in November 2004?

17 Which player turned out for Ferencvaros against Hearts and later played for Hibs?

18 Who were Hearts' first Champions League opponents?

19 Which four players have scored Champions League goals for the club?

20 Hearts have played against three teams from the same city in European competition – name the city?

Answers on page 61

Hearts Hotshots

Hearts' history is punctuated by players who could put the ball in the net. Barney Battles, Jimmy Wardhaugh and John Robertson are truly legends – not just at Hearts but can rightfully claim their places amongst the best goalscorers in Scottish football history. Here, we look at a few of the Gorgie goalgetters…

John Robertson

Few players command such respect around Tynecastle these days as John Robertson. Both as a player and manager, he has served the club with distinction and he has become synonymous with Hearts.

Robertson was not only a scorer of note but a scorer of noteworthy goals and established a rapport with the Hearts' fans that few have managed. If his spell as manager of the club was all too brief, many suspect he will be back in the hot seat at some stage.

His club record 214 league goals set him up alongside the club's all-time greats like Bobby Walker, Tommy Walker, Willie Bauld and Jimmy Wardhaugh. That his goals came in the modern era, is all the more remarkable.

Robertson was a prolific goalscorer even back in his primary school days in Edinburgh and took that habit all the way to the international stage where he won 16 caps for Scotland and scored eight times.

No doubt contributing to his popularity down Gorgie way was the fact that he managed to net a record 27 goals against Hibs and tormented the Easter Road side throughout his playing days.

He made his competitive debut in a 4-1 win over Queen of the South in 1982 and before too long was an integral part of the team. From 1983-84 to 1996-97, he led the club scoring charts apart from one season (in 1988-89 when he was at Newcastle United).

He took Hearts to the brink of the league title in 1986 with 20 goals in 34 appearances and, after scoring 31 goals in 1987-88, it was no surprise that Newcastle should lure him south. It was short-lived and Hearts paid a club record £750,000 to get him back not long afterwards.

He continued to serve the club well and won a Scottish Cup winner's medal in 1998 as an unused substitute in the famous win over Rangers at Celtic Park.

Robertson went on to play for Livingston before having management spells at Inverness Caledonian Thistle, Hearts, Ross County and Livingston.

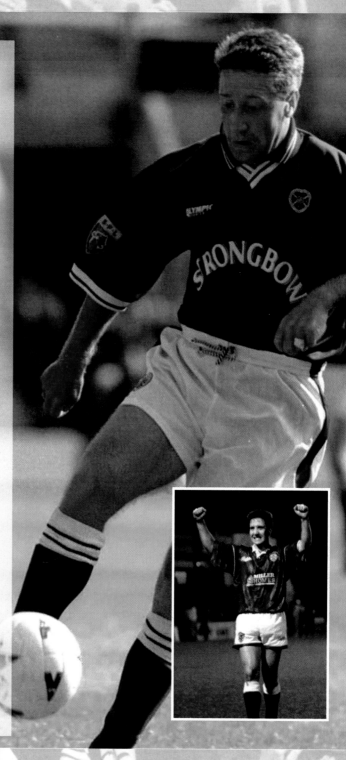

Jimmy Wardhaugh

Quite simply, the greatest goalscorer in Tynecastle history. If John Robertson eclipsed him in terms of league goals, "Robbo" could not come close in terms of overall goals as Wardhaugh bagged a remarkable 376 in just 519 matches.

A great all-round sportsman, Wardhaugh signed for Hearts at the age of 17 back in 1946 from Shaftesbury Park and it was obvious from the start that he thrived on the move as he netted on his debut in a 3-2 win over Celtic.

Yet there was not any great indication about how successful he was going to be after that instant hit as he played 11 more games in that first season and only managed one more goal.

It was obvious even in those early stages, however, that his phenomenal fitness would mean he could keep going for 90 minutes and he always seemed to have that extra yard of pace on defenders.

Good with both feet and also in the air, he was to grow in stature over the years as part of the great Hearts team of the late 1950s, early 1960s.

Playing alongside Willie Bauld and Alfie Conn he was at his most prolific, he netted 24 in season 1949-50 including four in one match against Clyde and then finished the club's top scorer the following season with 34 goals.

At one stage, with Bauld out through injury, he scored 27 goals in 28 matches and he went on to play a big part in Hearts' trophy haul over the next few seasons. He scored in the 1954 League Cup win over Motherwell and was Scotland's top scorer in 1957-58 when he shot Hearts to the league title with 37 goals.

He was capped twice by Scotland but left Hearts in 1959 when he was sold to Dunfermline at the age of 30 for a fee of £2,000, considerably more than then manager Dave McLean first paid for him.

Barney Battles

There can be few, Tynecastle fans who can boast that they saw Barney Battles in the flesh. Yet his name crops up in any record book on the club and he still warrants a regular mention in the Hearts' matchday magazine.

His goalscoring record was phenomenal, even given the fact that his career at Tynecastle occurred in the days when defences were not as well drilled as in today's game.

In 200 first-team appearances in maroon, Battles his 218 goals and, most notably, he hit 44 league goals in one season – 1930-31 – a record which has stood the test of time and has not been surpassed since.

Hearts beat off competition from Rangers and Celtic to land the Musselburgh-born striker when he returned to Scotland in 1928 after a successful spell in America, where he actually won an international cap.

A giant of a striker, it was patently clear he would score goals wherever he went, thus the stiff competition for his signature.

Hearts dug deep to offer him a £20 signing-on fee and paid him handsomely at £9 a week and the interest in him was such that 18,000 fans turned out just to watch his first trial game for Hearts. He did not let the crowd down, scoring four times.

He went on to make his league debut against Queen's Park at Hampden and his regular goalscoring exploits attracted attention from England with Arsenal one of the clubs taking a more than passing interest.

But Battles stayed at Tynecastle and would have undoubtedly scored more than the 44 he amassed in 1930-31 had he not missed several matches due to illness.

He was capped once for Scotland – against Wales at Hampden in 1931 – but had to retire from the game prematurely at the age of 30 due to injury.

Drew Busby

Drew Busby was hugely popular with the Hearts' supporters in the 1970s as he scored many vital goals and was a no-nonsense centre-forward.

Defenders hated playing against him because he was useful in the air but also strong on the ball and difficult to out-muscle. He always put in a full shift and defences knew they could never rest when up against him.

His early days were spent at Coventry City but he soon returned home where he had spells at Third Lanark and then Airdrie. It was with the latter that he made his name as he formed a formidable double-act with Drew Jarvie, who later went on to play for Aberdeen.

Hearts paid Airdrie £35,000 for him in the summer of 1973 and Busby was soon paying them back in the currency of goals. Linking well with Donald Ford in that first season, Hearts had one of the best teams in Scotland. The pair netted 45 goals between them and Ford went on to gain international recognition for Scotland. Hearts finished sixth in the league as they suffered a lack on consistency and also reached the last four of the Scottish Cup before losing out to Dundee United after a replay.

Busby was joint top scorer for Hearts with Willie Gibson in 1975-76 when he helped Hearts to the Scottish Cup final with a goal in the semi-final win over Dumbarton but the trophy was to elude the club.

Busby left the club at the end of the 1978-79 season after netting 84 competitive goals in his six years at Tynecastle. He went on to play for Toronto Blizzards in Canada before returning to play for Morton and Queen of the South.

Donald Ford

Donald Ford deserves his place in any list of great Tynecastle strikers. If he never won any silverware at the club, his 188 goals in 436 appearances came when the club was going through a difficult phase after the success of the early 1960s.

Signed as an amateur so he could pursue his studies as a chartered accountant, he broke into the side after Willie Wallace had joined Celtic. He was top scorer for the club for eight years in a row and went on to win three caps for his country.

There looked to be an early honour when he scored the only goal of a Scottish Cup quarter-final replay against Rangers as Hearts went on to reach the final and were huge favourites to beat Dunfermline. Unfortunately, it was the Fife team, with Alex Edwards pulling the strings in midfield, who won the trophy 3-1.

Ford played a big part in Hearts' successful runs in the Texaco Cup – a cross-border competition for English and Scottish teams who had missed out on Europe in the early 1970s. Hearts lost to Wolves in the 1971 final.

The centre-forward also enjoyed the rare distinction of scoring a hat-trick of penalties, in a game against Morton in 1973 which Hearts won 3-2.

Ford built up a strong partnership with Drew Busby and scored 29 goals in season 1973-74 as Hearts threatened to go the distance in the league but injuries and suspensions took their toll and the team eventually finished sixth.

He made his international debut against Czechoslovakia in Prague in a World Cup qualifying match in 1973 and went on to win further caps against West Germany and Wales.

Was selected by Willie Ormond for the Scotland squad for the World Cup finals in Germany in 1974 and travelled with the squad but was not involved in any of the games against Zaire, Brazil and Yugoslavia.

WORD SEARCH

G	E	F	T	N	A	L	L	O	W	N
S	G	D	W	A	B	R	O	P	T	L
J	O	O	F	H	A	M	N	T	Q	S
U	R	N	O	C	O	Y	O	R	K	S
B	D	R	I	A	E	Y	S	H	E	C
Y	O	A	U	L	B	H	T	I	M	S
R	N	O	T	L	I	M	A	H	T	J
Z	B	R	O	A	C	Y	W	O	Y	M
M	A	J	A	C	K	S	O	N	Y	C
H	R	T	C	H	L	L	A	C	H	N

Find these names in the word search. The words can go vertical, horizontal, diagonal or backwards.

1.	Brown
2.	Callachan
3.	Hamilton
4.	Gordon
5.	Watson
6.	Smith
7.	Jackson
8.	Hartley

What do these former Hearts players all have in common?

Answers on page 61

CIS Cup Review 2006-2007

Alloa Athletic	0	Hearts	4

Hibernian	1	Hearts	0

Juho Makela looked the Finnished article as he saw off Alloa with the perfect hat-trick at Recreation Park.

Makela scored with each boot and also his head as Hearts dominated from start to finish.

Alloa ended up with ten men after Chris Townsley was sent off late in the game.

Hearts re-cast their team from the weekend match against Motherwell with Makela getting a rare start, Steve Banks taking over in goal and Kestutis Ivaskevicius making his debut.

Makela served up warning of what was to come when he lashed a shot narrowly wide after just eight minutes.

He opened the scoring after 34 minutes when he was left unmarked in the area and he headed home a Takis Fyssas cross.

It gave Hearts some breathing space at half-time and the Finn added his second just half-a-minute after the restart when Neil McCann put him through and he slotted the ball home.

McCann almost got on the scoresheet himself shortly afterwards after being set up by Roman Bednar but his shot was cleared off the line by Steven McKeown.

Alloa tried to get back and the dangerous Ross Hamilton looped a header over Banks but substitute Alan Lithgow cleared off the line.

Townsley was sent off for a second yellow card in the 79th minute following a foul on Andrius Velicka.

Makela killed the game off three minutes later after Andrius Velicka flicked the ball on.

The striker's initial effort was saved by Allan Creer but he followed up to net the rebound.

Bruno Aguiar rounded off the scoring two minutes from time when he lobbed the ball over Creer to give Hearts an emphatic victory.

A first-half goal from Hibernian skipper Rob Jones settled a lack-lustre CIS Cup quarter-final at Easter Road.

Jones struck from a corner after 32 minutes when he prodded the ball past Craig Gordon from a Merouane Zemmama corner.

The goal gave John Collins victory in his first Edinburgh derby as a manager and the competition was eventually to provide him with his first trophy as Hibs progressed to the final to beat Kilmarnock.

It was a game of few chances but Christophe Berra made a great early stop to block a shot from Chris Killen as Hearts looked exposed at the back.

The New Zealand international striker then tested Gordon with a stinging shot from 20 yards but it was easily dealt with by the goalkeeper.

Hibs played their best football towards half-time and, after Jones put them in front, only the brilliance of Gordon denied them a second towards the interval.

Scott Brown exchanged passes with Zemmama but tried to be too precise with his finish and Gordon managed to stick out a boot to deflect the ball to safety.

David Murphy then saw a long-range shot curl wide but Gordon looked to have it covered.

Goalscorer Jones made his presence felt when his glancing header flew narrowly wide 10 minutes after the re-start but Hibs did not threaten too much after the break.

Berra made a great challenge to deny Killen again and then Guillaume Beuzelin went close with a chip from outside the area.

Hearts threatened at times on the break but, although they had plenty of possession, they found their rivals well organised at the back.

Killen and Steven Whittaker both had decent efforts in the closing stages but Gordon was never seriously threatened and the home side seemed content to play out time in the final minutes.

Gary Glen

Gary, a former pupil at Broxburn Academy, joined Hearts after coming through the club's successful youth system in 2006.

A local lad, born in Livingston on March 12 1990, Gary has featured for Scotland at youth level scoring against Northern Ireland and England in the 2005 Victory Shield.

Highly rated by the Hearts coaching staff, the striker earned his first involvement with the first team squad when he was named on the bench for the SPL match against Motherwell on 5 March 2007.

He made his senior debut as a substitute against Dundee United on 17 March 2007 replacing Michal Pospisil midway through the second half of the 4-0 victory.

This feat made him the third youngest ever first-team player for Hearts just five days short of his 17th birthday.

Sean Mackle

Sean is regarded as a true star of the future by the Hearts coaching staff and has earned a five year contract at the club after a successful first senior season which saw him begin his breakthrough to first-team football.

Born in Lurgan on April 10 1988, Sean qualifies to play for Scotland, Northern Ireland and the Republic of Ireland thanks to his Irish father and Scottish mother. He is currently a member of the successful Scotland Under-19 side.

Mackle joined Hearts from the Lurgan youth system in 2005. His first involvement with the first team squad came when he was an unused substitute in the SPL match against Motherwell on 5 March 2007.

Matej Rapnik

Slovenian centre-half Matej has been slated as one of the stars of the future at Tynecastle.

Born on February 24 1990 the teenager will begin his time at the club in the Under-19 side but is expected to progress quickly to the first team.

The left-sided defender signed a two-year agreement to join the club in July 2007.

He is already considered one to watch in his native Slovenia after shining as captain of the country's Under-17 side.

Matej, who comes from the Koroska Dravograd club, says that England captain and fellow centre-half is his footballing hero.

Eggert Jonsson

Eggert might have been born in Reykjavik, Iceland but he is a Hearts man through and through after joining the club's youth system in July 2005. As soon as he turned 18 he put pen to paper on a professional contract with the club signalling his intent to stay at Tynecastle in the future.

Born on August 18 1988 Eggert is capable of playing as either a defensive midfielder or central defender.

Jónsson made his debut as a 15 year old for Fjarðabyggð in Iceland. After that he trained with Þór Akureyri.

He made his debut for Hearts on the 20 September 2006, appearing as a substitute in the impressive 4-0 CIS Cup victory over Alloa Athletic.

He made his home debut as a substitute in Hearts 1-0 win over Inverness Caledonian Thistle in February 2007, one of five first-team appearances he made in the 2006-2007 season.

Branimir Kostodinov

Bulgarian Branimir is set to make the breakthrough to Hearts' senior side after impressing in pre-season training in 2007.

The pacey striker joined the club in 2006 but spent the 2006-07 season out on loan with Tynecastle Amateurs.

Born on March 4 1989 in Veliko Tarnovo, Bulgaria, Branimir started his career at FC Slavia Sofia scoring 24 goals in just 23 games in the U17 Youth League in the 2003-03 season

In 2004 Branimir moved to Austria to join FC Lask Linz where he continued to impress with 16 goals in as many games in the Austrian U19 league.

In 2006 Branimir won his first cap for the Bulgarian U21 side.

After scoring in a pre-season match against BV Cloppenberg in July 2007 Branimir has made his mark on the Hearts squad.

Hearts have a formidable derby record at Tynecastle but Easter Road has also been the backdrop to some of the club's most memorable derby days. Here we look at some memorable matches against our oldest rivals…

April 1 2007	
Premier League	
Hibernian 0	Hearts 1

Marius Zaliukas is assured his place in Edinburgh derby folklore after giving Hearts a victory that breathed new life into their season.

There was much wailing and gnashing of teeth after the 4-0 home defeat by Dundee United in their previous match and Hearts needed a result on the back of their training camp in Hamburg.

With Hibs having crushed Kilmarnock at Hampden to win the CIS Cup on their last outing, this was the opportunity to parade the trophy in front of their fans after beating their arch-rivals. On April Fool's Day, Zaliukas tore up that particular script.

Hearts managed to get their tactics spot on as they soaked up some early Hibs' pressure before hitting them with the classic sucker-punch with just nine minutes left.

Craig Gordon made a couple of decent saves from Steven Fletcher and David Murphy in the first half-hour but there were not too many goalmouth incidents in what was not one of the better derbies.

But it was Hearts who made the breakthrough. Andy

McNeil was at fault when he failed to deal with an Andy Driver cross and the ball broke to Zaliukas who steered it into the net. It sparked wild celebrations from the Hearts' end that went on long after the final whistle and rather soured the occasion for the home side.

November 3 2002	
Premier League	
Hibernian 1	Hearts 2

Hearts' Stamped their authority over their Edinburgh neighbours with this last-gasped victory. It was former Middlesbrough midfield player Phil Stamp who snatched an injury-time goal to give Hearts the most unlikely of victories.

Such was his celebrations behind the Hibs' goal that he was shown his second yellow card by referee Willie Young and sent off but nothing could wipe the smile off Stamp's face.

Hibs, who had won their last five league games, had been seeking revenge for the 5-1 mauling at Tynecastle earlier in the season. It all looked to be going according to plan when Mixu Paatelainen bundled them ahead nine minutes from half-time after Ian Murray had headed down a Jarko Wiss corner.

But Hearts' boss Craig Levein made a significant change when he sent on Neil Janczyk and he was to prove the provider of two late goals.

He supplied the 86th-minute cross for makeshift striker Kevin McKenna to head the equaliser and it looked as if Hearts had salvaged a point.

But it was to prove even sweeter for the Gorgie faithful when Janczyk picked out Stamp who steered the ball beyond Nick Colgan to complete a dramatic turnaround.

January 1 1997	
Premier League	
Hibernian 0	Hearts 4

Hearts achieved their biggest league win at Easter Road in 36 years with a comprehensive New Year's Day win. Jim Jefferies' side were on the rise and were to mount a strong challenge in the league as well as going on to win the Scottish Cup.

It was a game which marked John Robertson's 25th goal against Hibs (he was to go on to score a record 27 against the Easter Road side) as he beat Jim Leighton after 33 minutes and Hearts' cause was helped five minutes later when Hibs' defender Andy Millen was sent off.

It gave Hearts numerical advantage in the second half and they punished Jim Duffy's side with three goals. Jim Hamilton made it 2-0 after 62 minutes with an opportunist effort before Colin Cameron made it three a couple of minutes later.

It was one-way traffic after this as Hearts' lay siege to the Hibs' goal and Leighton made a couple of good saves to keep the Gorgie side at bay.

But Hamilton nabbed his second and Hearts' fourth three minutes from time to complete a great afternoon for the club.

February 20 1994	
Scottish Cup	
Hibernian 1	Hearts 2

Wayne Foster proved that timing is everything in derbies as he gave Hearts a stunning fourth round cup win at Easter Road.

The substitute scored one of the most famous derby goals in modern times when he netted the winner with just three minutes left, racing onto a through ball from Gary Mackay to beat Jim Leighton with a low shot.

He immediately went to the fans behind the goal to celebrate and left favourites Hibs on the ropes.

Sandy Clark was Hearts' manager for this Sunday fixture and he could scarcely have had a better start when hammer-of-Hibs John Robertson scored after only two minutes when he converted a Tosh McKinlay cross.

Hibs responded and Keith Wright headed an equaliser before the interval from a Michael O'Neill cross.

There was little to choose between the teams but Kevin McAllister struck a post for Hibs in the second

half as the home side threatened to snatch it.

Just when it looked as if the match was heading for a Tynecastle replay, Foster – who had replaced Robertson – came out of nowhere to score the winner and send Hearts into a last eight tie with Rangers.

January 2 1991	
Premier League	
Hibernian 1	Hearts 4

Gary Mackay has cause to remember this New Year clash as he managed to score at both ends in a memorable encounter which was screened live on television.

The game came sandwiched between matches with the Old Firm and Joe Jordan was seeking to make his mark in what was his first derby at Easter Road.

The manager need not have worried as Hearts were at their most commanding against a Hibs side struggling under Alex Miller.

Tosh McKinlay fired a spectacular opener as he beat Andy Goram from 25 yards after just eight minutes and Dave McPherson added a second goal shortly afterwards to put Hearts in control.

Mackay then took a hand in things as he squeezed home a third goal shortly before half-time after John Robertson and Goram had tussled for the ball and the Hearts' fans could hardly believe the one-sided nature of the game.

Hibs' task was made more difficult after half-time when Pat McGinlay was sent off but they did get a goal back when Mackay sent the ball into his own net while attempting to clear.

But there was to be no fightback and Craig Levein completed the scoring late on to give Hearts a handsome victory.

September 5 1964	
Scottish League	
Hibernian 3	Hearts 5

Hearts were to come within a whisker of the league title in 1965 and one of their most memorable victories of that season was an eight-goal thriller at Easter Road.

Hearts had already shown themselves capable in the scoring stakes by firing eight past Airdrie earlier in the season and beating Partick Thistle 4-3 in the match before visiting Easter Road.

Alan Gordon – later to join Hibs - headed Hearts in front from a Tommy Traynor cross and Willie Wallace made it 2-0 before half-time with a shot from the edge of the penalty area.

Jim Scott pulled a goal back for Hibs early in the second half but Gordon restored Hearts' two-goal cushion shortly afterwards.

Scott kept Hibs' hopes alive by adding his second to make it 2-3 but, with neither defence looking particularly convincing, it was Hearts who stepped up a gear.

Tommy White and Traynor both scored to give Hearts a 5-2 advantage and, although Neil Martin pulled a goal back for the home side, by then it was much too late to affect the outcome.

Hearts took confidence from the result and went another 14 matches unbeaten before losing to Kilmarnock six days before Christmas, a result which was to prove significant on the final day of the season.

April 1 1960	
Scottish League	
Hibernian 1	Hearts 5

Hearts were on their way to their second league title in three years as they outclassed Hibs in Leith. In a season when the team also won the League Cup and scored 102 goals in the league, few could live with them.

Indeed, only Hibs (106) managed to score more league goals that season but could only finish a distant seventh in the table.

After securing a 2-2 draw at Tynecastle earlier in the season, much was expected of Hibs with England international striker Joe Baker proving a handful for most defences and 54,000 packed into Easter Road.

But Jimmy Milne kept him quiet as Hearts, three points clear at the top of the league, dominated.

Alex Young, who finished top Hearts' scorer that season with 28 goals, opened the scoring after only seven minutes and, 13 minutes later, an own goal from Jackie Plenderleith had left Hibs with an uphill struggle.

Nine minutes into the second half, Young made it 3-0 before Bobby Johnstone pulled a goal back for the home side. But, within a minute of Johnstone's counter, Young had completed his hat-trick to make it 4-1.

To make matter worse for the home side, their former favourite Gordon Smith then added a fifth after 72 minutes to complete the scoring.

Maroon Five Quiz (page 16)

1. Ibrahim Tall.
2. Mark de Vries
3. Willie Gibson (2), Roy Kay, Jim Brown and Drew Busby
4. John Colquhoun
5. Willie Bauld
6. Hibernian
7. Mauricio Pinilla – the first goal in the 4-1 win over Inverness Caledonian Thistle.
8. Freddie Glidden
9. 515
10. Tennent's Sixes
11. Kilmarnock
12. Paul Hartley – in the 55th minute!
13. Calum Elliot
14. Dunfermline – in the Scottish Cup tie at East End Park
15. Lantana Tallinn
16. Gary McSwegan
17. 1895
18. Neil Berry
19. Hearts 4 Hibs 3
20. 1925

Wordsearch (Page 23)

				S			S	
	G			M		N		R
	A			I		W	R	E
	R		M	T		O		T
	L		E	H	U	R		T
	A	I		S		B		A
	N		S				W	
	D	R	E	K	L	A	W	
		T		H	G	U	O	R	B

Euro Quiz (page 46)

1. Ian Crawford v Standard Liege in 1958
2. Standard Liege – 2-1 at Tynecastle in 1958 but Hearts went out 6-3 on aggregate
3. Union St Gilloise of Luxembourg in the old Inter-Cities Faris Cup in 1961. Hearts won 5-1 on aggregate
4. SV Hamburg on an 8-3 aggregate
5. John Robertson in a 2-2 draw with Paris St Germain at Tynecastle in 1984
6. Dukla Prague
7. Mike Galloway
8. Bologna on a 4-3 aggregate in the second round of the UEFA Cup
9. Glyn Snodin
10. Arie Haan
11. John Colquhoun and John Robertson
12. Red Star Belgrade in the Cup-Winners' Cup in 1996
13. Steven Pressley, Gordan Petric and Colin Cameron (pen)
14. Mark de Vries
15. It meant Hearts were the first British team to qualify for the new group stages of the UEFA Cup
16. Robbie Neilson
17. Thomas Sowunmi
18. Bosnian side Siroki Brijeg
19. Ibrahim Tall, Roman Bednar, Saulius Mikoliunas… and an own goal from Siroki Brijeg's Branimir Anic
20. Prague – Dukla, Slavia and Sparta

Wordsearch (Page 51)

				N						
	G		W	A						
	O	O		H			N			
	R			C		Y	O			
B	D			A	E	S	S			
	O			L		H	T	I	M	S
	N	O	T	L	I	M	A	H		
		R		A			W			
	A	J	A	C	K	S	O	N		
H										

Common link: All of the players also played for Hibernian at some stage in their career.